Rimbles

A BOOK OF CHILDREN'S
CLASSIC GAMES,
RHYMES, SONGS, AND
SAYINGS

BOOKS BY PATRICIA EVANS

JUMP ROPE RHYMES

HOPSCOTCH

JACKS

WHO'S IT

STICKS AND STONES

THE MYCOPHAGISTS' BOOK (MUSHROOM COOKERY)

AN ALPHABET BOOK

BOOKS ILLUSTRATED BY PATRICIA EVANS

HOW TO TELL A STORY *by Josephine Gardner*

FIRST DUET *by Henry Evans*

WESTERN BIBLIOGRAPHIES *by Henry Evans*

WINEMAKING IN CALIFORNIA *by Ernest Peninou and Sidney Greenleaf*

DRAWINGS AND DIAGRAMS BY GIOIA FIAMMENGHI

1961 DOUBLEDAY & COMPANY, INC.

GARDEN CITY, NEW YORK

Rimbles

A BOOK OF CHILDREN'S CLASSIC GAMES,

RHYMES, SONGS, AND SAYINGS

BY PATRICIA EVANS

Library of Congress Catalog Card Number 61-9504

Printed in the United States of America

Designed by Alma Reese Cardi

First Edition

CONTENTS

INTRODUCTION

These rhymes are called rimbles from the French word rimailler, *the verb meaning to write doggerel as opposed to* rimer, *to write verse. All in this book were collected from children except for a few from older people, in many parts of California, Oregon, Washington, Colorado, Indiana, Delaware, and New York during the years from 1945 to 1960. Many of these games were collected from children in San Francisco. I want to thank all of the children who co-operated by teaching me the games they play and the things they say. Happily, in San Francisco, there are children from all over the world.*

The compiler will be very grateful for any additions or corrections, sent to her in care of the publisher. At this time she sincerely thanks all those who have contributed to this volume or helped with its production, especially Henry and Judy.

Book One

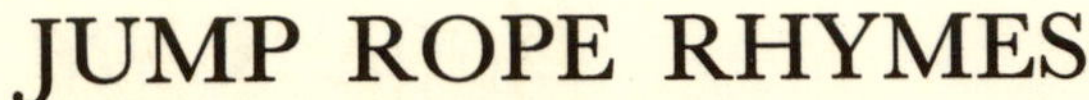

JUMP ROPE RHYMES

Jumping rope is one of the oldest games in the world. Once, when people planted their crops in the spring, they would have a celebration with songs and jumping contests. They believed that their crops would grow only as high as they could jump. We still jump rope more in the spring than at any other time of the year.

Rope jumping was traditionally a game played on

Good Friday. One early rhyme was *Pop Goes the Weasel.* The *earliest* rhyme I can find goes:

Andy Pandy
Sugardy Candy
French Almond, Rock.

This is clearly the one used now:

Amos and Andy
Sugar and Candy
I spy up

Amos and Andy
Sugar and Candy
I spy down

Amos and Andy
Sugar and Candy
I spy OUT.

Jumping rope was, and is, used for many kinds of fortune-telling: whom will I marry? how many children will I have? how long will I live? etc. Other rhymes test how long or how fast a person can jump, sometimes answering a question at the same time.

Some of the rhymes tell a story and mention different movements. As these are said, the jumper is supposed to do them, without changing the rhythm. When a rhyme ends with the word "out," the jumper has to run out of the rope.

Two characters who appear in many jump rope rhymes are the *Spanish Dancer* and *The Lady with the Alligator Purse.* I'd like to find out who they really are, because all of the rhymes, even if they appear to be nonsense, are completely logical in their origins.

Following are some of the terms used in jumping rope when the rope is turned by two players for the others to jump:

BABY ROPE: The rope is swung back and forth in an arc but is not turned over the jumper's head.

BLUE BELLS: Same as Baby Rope.

OVERS: The rope is turned around under the jumper's feet and over her head.

HOT, OF HOTS: Rope is turned rapidly.

PEPPERS: Rope is turned as fast as possible.

EVER-ENDER: A rope turner who decides (or is told) to turn the rope all the time without joining in the jumping.

NEVER-ENDER: Same as Ever-ender.

FRONT DOORS: To run into the turning rope from the side where it turns down toward you and you are in the middle before you make your first jump.

BACK DOORS: To run into the rope when it is being turned the other way, coming up and over, so you have to jump over it to get into the middle.

DOUBLE ROPE, OF DOUBLES: Two ropes are used, one end of each in each turner's hand. They can be turned either toward or away from each other. Sometimes called Double Dutch.

TWIRLS: Only one turner, who doubles the rope to make it heavier, holds both ends in one hand, and then twirls herself and the rope with her. The players are in a circle, jumping the rope as it reaches each. This does not last very long because the one in the center gets dizzy.

OUT: When the rhyme ends with the word *out* the jumper runs out of the rope to make room for the next player.

SALT, VINEGAR, MUSTARD, PEPPER: Often used as a rhyme or at the end of a rhyme, these four words mean successively faster speeds of jumping.

WINDING THE CLOCK: Turning around and around while you jump.

BAKING BREAD: Picking up a stone or something while jumping.

And here are some of the games played with a jump rope:

FOLLOW THE FOX: The first player to jump through does whatever she wants to, or can do. The others imitate the first one until all have had a turn. Then the "fox" does something else, or is replaced by the next in line who becomes the "fox." A kind of Follow the Leader.

SCHOOL: The first one runs through the rope without jumping and the others follow. Next time around they each jump once, the next time twice, and so on. Of course if anyone misses, she has to take an end of the rope. The ends are taken alternately unless there is an Ever-Ender.

HEIGHTS: The two holding the ends of the rope do not turn it but at first just let it lie on the ground. After each player has jumped over it in turn, the rope is raised a few inches. The players must jump higher each time the rope is raised.

A player drops out when she wants to or if she misses.

This game is called by several different names: BIRTHDAY MONTHS; SUNNY, SUNNY WEATHER; or RAINY, RAINY WEATHER. The point is that when your birthday month is mentioned you run into the rope and jump with the others. It sometimes can get quite crowded. You run out when your birthday month is mentioned the second time. It begins:

All in together, girls.
How is the weather, girls?
January, February, March
(and so on through the months).

At the end:

All out together, girls.
How is the weather, girls?
(and repeat the months)

Or:

Sunny, sunny weather
All come in together.
January, February, etc. . . .

and at the end:

Rainy, rainy weather
All go out together

and then the months.

You can always jump alone holding the rope in your hands and turning it over your own head. You can jump either forward or backward, with rhymes or without, on one foot, with arms crossed, or to test how long you can jump. Two can jump this way together, with one of them turning the rope. Now the rhymes begin:

Apple, peach, punkin pie.
How many days before I die?
1 2 3

Ice cream soda water
Gingerale pop
Cameron, Cameron,
Always on the top.
Stand there on their heads,
Stand there on their feet.
Cameron, Cameron,
Can't be beat.

Rosy apple, Mama's little tot,
Tell me the name of your sweetheart.
A B C

Cinderella, dressed in yella,
Ran downstairs to meet her fella.
On the way her garter busted;
How many people were disgusted?
1 2 3

In the next one, as in all those in which E V I V (*EEVIE IVIE*) occurs, the rope is first swung back and forth, Baby Rope, and on the word *over* is turned over the jumper's head.

E V I V over
The kettle's boiling over.

Tinkle bells and cockle shells
E V I V over.
Mary Mack, dressed in black,
Silver buckles down her back.

Jack be nimble, Jack be quick,
Jack jump over the candlestick.
How many times did he jump?
1 2 3

Denny, Denny, [name of jumper]
Do you love her?
Yes. No. Maybe so. Yes.

Way down South where bananas grow
An ant stepped on an elephant's toe.
The elephant cried with tears in his eyes,
"Why don't you pick on someone your size?"

Grace, Grace, dressed in lace,
Went upstairs to powder her face.
How many boxes did she use?
1 2 3

My mother sent me to the store, (Baby Rope)
And this is what she sent me for: (Overs)
Salt, vinegar, mustard, pepper. (Peppers)

Oh, say, kid,
What do you think I did?
I upset the cradle
And out fell the kid.
The kid began to holler;
I took him by the collar;
Collar broke loose
And I got the deuce.

When I went down to grandfather's farm
A billy goat chased me around the barn.
He chased me up a sycamore tree,
And this is what he said to me:
"Down by the water where the green grass grows
There sits Susan [name of next jumper] *as sweet as a rose."*

Virginia had a baby.
His name was Tiny Tim.
She put him in a bathtub
To teach him how to swim.
He floated up the river,
He floated down the lake,
And now Virginia's baby
Has the stomach ache.

Chicken on the railroad,
Chicken on the fence,
Johnny got a haircut,
Fifteen cents.

I love coffee, I love tea,
I love the boys and the boys love me.
Tell your mother to hold her tongue;
She had a fellow when she was young.
Tell your father to do the same;
He had a girl and he changed her name.

This one is said as a dialogue, the first part being taken by the rope turners and the children waiting their turn, the second by the jumper:

—There came two Spaniards just from Spain
Talking about your daughter Jane.
—My daughter Jane is yet too young
To be controlled by anyone.
—Be she young or be she old
For all the money she must be sold.
—Then don't let her gallop
Don't let her trot
Don't let her play
In the mustard pot.

This house to let,
No rent to pay,
Knock at the door
And run away.

Butterfly, Butterfly, turn around, 'round, 'round,
Butterfly, Butterfly, touch the ground, ground, ground.

Butterfly, Butterfly, throw a kiss, kiss, kiss,
Butterfly, Butterfly, get out before you miss, miss, miss.

Anthy Maria jumped in the fire.
The fire too hot, she jumped in the pot.
The pot was too black, she jumped in a crack.
The pot was soon over, she jumped in some clover.
Clover's too sweet, she kicked up her feet.
Feet was soon over, she cried 1 2 3,
Jumped in a tree.
The tree was so high she couldn't go higher.
'Long came a breeze, blew her away.

In the next rhyme the jumper misses at each *Miss:*

I know a little lady
But her name is Miss.
She went around the corner
To buy some fish.
She met a little fellow
And she gave him a kiss.
I know a little lady
But her name is Miss.

In the following, on the first wiggle-waggle the jumper turns sharply to the right, and if jumping alone twists the rope with her; on the second wiggle-waggle repeat to the left.

Jelly in the dish,
Jelly in the dish,
Wiggle-waggle
Wiggle-waggle
Jelly in the dish.

During the next rhyme repeat each list, Peppers, until an answer is found, and then continue.

Mississippi lives by the shore;
She has children three and four,
The oldest one is twenty-four.
She shall marry
Tinker, tailor, soldier, sailor,

Rich man, poor man, beggar man, thief,
Doctor, lawyer, Indian chief.
Her shoes will be
Wood, leather, high heel, low heel, sandals, wooden.
Her dress will be made of
Silk, satin, cotton, batten, rags.
Her house will be
Big house, little house, pigpen, barn.
Her rings shall be made of
Diamonds, rubies, emeralds, glass.
How many children will she get?
1 2 3
And now you're married you must obey,
You must be true in every way.
You must be kind, you must be good,
And make your husband chop the wood.

And what is your fortune?

A gift? A beau? A friend? A foe? A journey to go?

Mother, Mother, I am ill.
Call the doctor over the hill.
In came the doctor.
In came the nurse.
In came the lady
With the alligator purse.
"Measles," said the doctor.
"Mumps," said the nurse.
"Nothing," said the lady
With the alligator purse.

Old Mother Whittlehouse
Had a big fit
First she did the merry-go-round
And then she did the split.

Sally Rand
Has lost her fan.
Give it back,
You naughty man.

The wind, the wind, the wind blows high,
It blows Mary through the sky.
She is fair and she is pretty
She is the girl from the tin can city.
She can play the piano, 1 2 3
Mary, Mary, who is she?
Johnny, Johnny says he loves her.
Off they go with a kiss, kiss, kiss.
He took her to the courtyard,
Asked her, "Will you marry me?"
Yes. No. Maybe so. Yes. No. Maybe so.

In this the rope is swung Blue Bells, high at first and then lower and lower:

Christopher Columbus
Sailed the ocean blue
In fourteen hundred
And ninety-two.

Old Mr. Kelly had a pimple on his belly,
His wife cut it off and made it into jelly.

I was standing on the corner,
Not doing any harm.
Along came a policeman
And took me by the arm.
He took me around the corner
And he rang a little bell.
Along came a police car
And took me to my cell.
I woke up in the morning
And looked up on the wall.
The cooties and the bedbugs
Were having a game of ball.
The score was six to nothing,
The bedbugs were ahead.
The cooties hit a home run
And knocked me out of bed.

An Ender's rhyme:

Everybody, everybody,
Come on in.
The first one misses
Gonna take my end.

I won't go to Macy's
Any more, more, more.
There's a big fat policeman
At the door, door, door.
He takes you by the collar
And he makes you pay a dollar.
I won't go to Macy's
Any more, more, more.

With a line of children coming up to jump, you have to get in on time; you also have to push the other jumper out—all on the one jump to the word "push."

Down the Mississippi
Where the steamboats
PUSH

House to rent, inquire within.
As I move out, let Judy [name of next jumper] *move in.*

My mother, your mother,
Lived across the way.
Sixteen-seventeen East Broadway.
Every night they'd have a fight,
And this is what they'd say:
Boys are rotten
Made of dirty cotton.
Girls are dandy
Made of sugar candy.
Acka-backa, soda cracker
Acka-backa-boo.
Acka-backa, soda cracker
Out goes you.

Acka-backa, soda cracker,
Does your father chew tobacco?
Yes. No. Maybe So. Yes. No, etc.

Here, the rope is turned by two people. A long line of children run through the rope jumping. On the word "time" the jumper runs out and the next one runs in. If you don't get in on time, it's a miss.

Keep the kettle boiling
In on time.

This one is the same as the last one in plan, just different words.

Keep the kettle boiling
Empty rope's a miss.

Ice cream soda
Delaware Punch
Tell me the name
Of your honey bunch.
A B C

Charlie Chaplin
Went to France
To teach the ladies
How to dance.
First the heel
And then the toe
Left foot forward
Out you go.

Or:

Do the splits
And around you go.

Little Orphan Annie
Hops on one foot, one foot.
Little Orphan Annie
Hops on two feet, two feet.
Little Orphan Annie
Hops on three feet, three feet.
Little Orphan Annie
Hops on four feet, four feet.
Little Orphan Annie hops out.

Johnnie made a touchdown.
Johnnie made a basketball.
Johnnie made an OUT.

I was in the kitchen
Doing a little switching.
Along came [name of next jumper]
And pushed me out.

On the hillside,
Stands a lady,
All she wants
Is gold and silver.
All she wants
Is the pretty little girl.
Jump in the pretty little girl.
Jump out the ugly little girl.

Postman, postman
Do your duty.
Here comes [name of girl jumping]
The American Beauty.
She can do the rhumba
She can do the splits,
She can pull her pretty dress
Right up to her hips.

Poor old lady,
She swallowed a fly.
Poor old lady,
She's going to die.
Poor old lady,
She swallowed a cat.
Imagine that!
Swallowing a cat!
Poor old lady,
She's going to die.
Poor old lady,
She swallowed a dog.
What a hog, to swallow a dog!
Poor old lady,
She's going to die.
Poor old lady,
She swallowed a horse.
She died, of course!

Down by the river
Where the green grass grows,
There sat [name of girl jumping]
Sweet as a rose.
She sang, she sang,
She sang so sweet,
Along came [name of her boy-friend]
And kissed her on the cheek.
How many kisses did she get?
1 2 3

Cinderella, dressed in yellow,
Went upstairs to kiss her fellow.
How many kisses did she get?
1 2 3

Charlie Chaplin
Went to France
To teach the girls
The hula-hula dance.
First on the heel,
Then on the toe,
Round and round and round you go.
Salute to the Captain
Bow to the Queen
And turn your back
On the dirty submarine.

I love coffee
I love tea
I love the boys
And the boys love me.
A B C

Old Man Lazy, drives me crazy. (Baby Rope)
Up the ladder, (Overs)
Down the ladder, (Reverse Rope; Overs)
Old Man Lazy. (Baby Rope)

Hitler, Hitler,
I've been thinking,
What on earth have
You been drinking?
Smells like whisky,
Tastes like wine,
Oh, my gosh!
It's iodine!

Order in the court,
The Judge is eating beans.
His wife is in the bathtub
Counting submarines.

I went down town to see Miss Brown.
She gave me a nickle to buy a pickle.
The pickle was sour so I bought a flower.
The flower was dead so I bought some thread.
The thread was thin so I bought a pin.
The pin was sharp so I bought a harp.
And on this harp I played:
Spanish dancer, do the splits,
Spanish dancer, give a high kick.
Spanish dancer, turn around.
Spanish dancer, touch the ground.

Teddy bear, Teddy bear,
Walking up the stairs.
Teddy bear, Teddy bear,
Won't you say your prayers?
Teddy bear, Teddy bear,
Turn out the light.
Teddy bear, Teddy bear,
Say good night.

I went downtown
To alligator round.
Sat on the fence
And the fence broke down.
Alligator caught me
By the seat of my pants,
And made me do
The hula-hula dance.

On every *sir,* touch your toe.

May I come in, sir?
No, sir. Why, sir?
Cause I got a cold, sir.
Where did you get your cold, sir?
At the North Pole, sir.
Whatcha doing there, sir?
Catching Polar Bears, sir.
How many Polar Bears did you catch?
1 2 3 (Peppers)

Johnny gave me apples
Johnny gave me pears
Johnny gave me fifteen cents
And kissed me on the stairs.
I'd rather wash the dishes
I'd rather scrub the floor
I'd rather kiss the dirty boy
Behind the kitchen door.

I was standing on the corner
Chewing a piece of gum.
Along came Sylvia
And asked for some.
Why you dirty little beggar!
Does your mother know you're out?
With your hands in your pockets
And your shirttail out?

I was born in a frying pan.
Just you see how old I am.
1 2 3

Little Miss Pinky
Dressed in blue,
Died last night
At half past two.
As she died
She told me this:
Darn that rope
That made me miss.

Miss on purpose.

Mabel, Mabel,
Set the table
And don't forget
The red-hot peppers.

Rope is turned *Peppers* (very fast), without counting.

In, spin
Let Judy come in
Out, spout
Let Judy go out.

Old Mother Rich,
Fell in a ditch,
Picked up a rotten apple,
And thought she was rich.

Last night and the night before
Twenty-four robbers were at my door.
I went downstairs to let them in,
They hit me on the head with a rolling pin.
I went upstairs to get my gun,
You ought to seen those robbers run.

Fudge, fudge
Tell the Judge
Mama's got a newborn baby.
It ain't no girl
It ain't no boy
It's just a newborn baby.
Wrap it up in tissue paper.
Send it down the elevator.
First floor. Stop.
Second floor. Stop.
Third floor. Stop,
And throw the baby
O U T.

Down by the river,
Down by the sea,
Johnny broke a bottle
And he blamed it on me.
I told Ma,
Ma told Pa,
Johnny got a licking
So ha! ha! ha!
How many lickings
Did Johnny get?
1 2 3

1 2 3 O' Lary
My first name is Mary.
Don't you think that I look cute,
In my papa's bathing suit?

For, for, for, for Sherry.
In come Judy at the door.
Judy is a lady
That we never saw before,
So we don't need Sherry any more.

In this one the rope is turned by two people, and two people are jumping at the same time. As each number is called, the jumpers exchange places in the rope, without missing a jump.

Changing bedrooms
Number one
Changing bedrooms
Number two
Changing bedrooms
Number three
etc.

Spanish dancer,
Do the splits.
Spanish dancer,
Give a high kick.
Spanish dancer,
Take a sip of wine.
Close your eyes
And count to nine.

My father was a butcher,
My mother cut the meat.
And I'm a little wienie,
That runs around the street.
How many times
Did I run around the street?
1 2 3

Mother, Mother, I am ill.
Send for the doctor over the hill.
Doctor, Doctor will I die?
Yes you must and so must I.
How many years will I live?
1 2 3

Salome was a dancer,
She danced before the king.
And every time she danced,
She wiggled everything.
"Stop," said the king,
"You can't do that in here."
Salome said, "Baloney,"
And kicked the chandelier.

Blue bells, cockle shells,
Evey Ivy Overs (Baby Rope)
Here comes the teacher (Overs to end)
With a big fat stick.
You better get ready
For arithmetic.
1 and 1 are 2
2 and 2 are 4
4 and 4 are 8
Better get ready for spelling.
D O G spells dog
C A T spells cat
O U T spells out.

Book Two

HOPSCOTCH

A long time ago there was a king named Minos who lived on the island of Crete. A monster was there called the Minotaur. He was half-man and half-bull and was in the habit of eating young people. So King Minos had a labyrinth or maze built and he put the monster in it. Then he made the city of Athens send their most beautiful young men and maidens to be the Minotaur's food. Finally one brave Athenian youth killed the monster and married the daughter of King Minos. They went back to

Athens and there was a big celebration. Lines were made on the ground like the maze and people danced through it. This is said to be the start of HOPSCOTCH.

Whether or not this is true, it is still interesting. But what is even more interesting is the fact that hopscotch is played all over the world. People say that hopscotch started in Greece, where the Romans learned it, who carried the game to England, whence it came to America. But we find it played in Burma, India, Japan, and other lands in early times as well as now. Which shows, since playing is one of the most important things we do, how much alike all peoples really are.

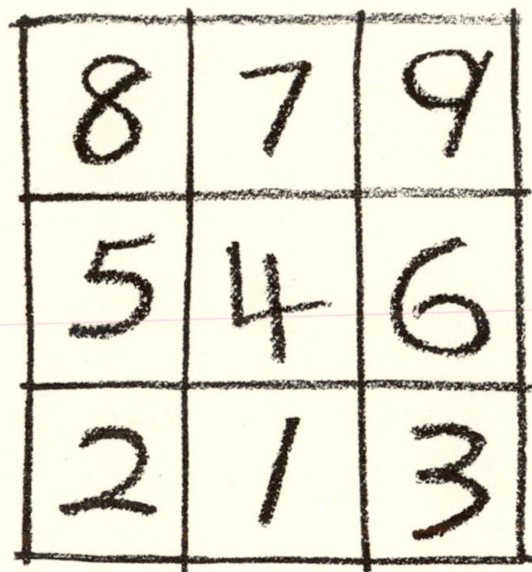

It is certainly an ancient game. In the old Forum in Rome there are still hopscotch diagrams scratched in the pavement. Pliny (who died in the year 79) tells of the boys in his time playing a round hopscotch. Later, Christians thought the game meant the progress of the soul from earth to heaven and called the last square *paradise.* In Norway today hopscotch is called HOP IN PARADISE. That is why the last square is sometimes rounded, to represent the dome of Heaven, even if we call it *Home* or *Radish* as we do in this game:

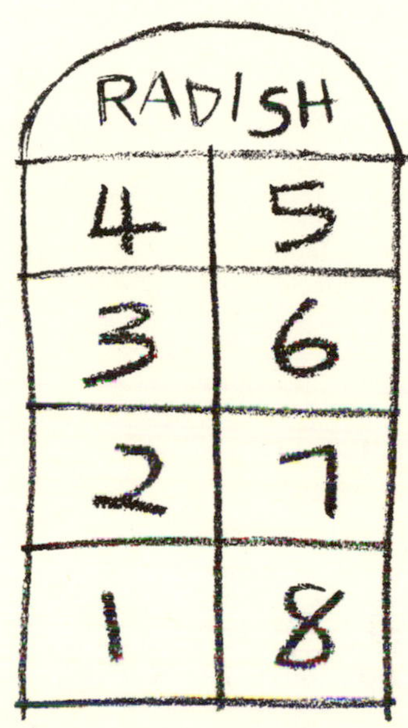

In the game of RADISH, a tor is called a *potsie* and instead of hopping, a kind of dancing step is used, a sideways skip. Throw your potsie into 1,* and start through the game at 8. Put your right foot in 8 and then while you put your left foot in 8, your right foot goes into 7, and so on around. When you get to Radish you can rest on both feet. When you get to 1, put your right foot in, pick

* Numbers, like 1, 2, and 3 have been used all through this book, but of course you know that when they're said, they're "Onesies, Twosies, and Threesies" and like that.

up your potsie, then put your left foot in while your right foot goes out. Go through the whole game the same way, except when you throw your potsie into 5, 6, 7, and 8, you start at 1. You have to go through all eight squares in the same turn; if you miss you have to start at 1 again.

After you get through you stand at the beginning and close your eyes tight and throw your potsie at Radish. Then you ask, "Radish?" If you got it in your friends answer, "Radish." Then you walk up to Radish, left foot in 1 and right foot in 8, and ask "Radish?" If you didn't step on a line, your friends answer "Radish." Then you step to 2 and 7 and ask again, and so on until you get to Radish. Then you feel around and pick up your potsie without opening your eyes. If you touch a line it's a miss and you have to wait your turn to start this part again. If you haven't missed, you walk back the same way, asking at each step and keeping your eyes closed. If you get through this part without touching or stepping on a line, you've won a game. You can keep score of how many games each one wins.

In early England the stone (or tor, or potsie, or pick, or scotch, or dump, or pally-ully) was kicked from one square to the next, as the player hopped, and not thrown as it is now. Of course if it was kicked so it landed on a line or if a player's foot touched a line in the kicking or hopping, it was a miss just as it is now. ("Step on a crack, break your mother's back.") After kicking the stone while hopping through the squares, the next game was played by carrying the stone on the palm of the hand while hopping, then on the back of the hand. Next the head was tipped back, eyes closed, and a smooth, flat stone was carried on one eye. This was the hardest and most dangerous of all. In the next game the players bent over and it was carried on the back, then on one shoulder. At the end of each game the player had to toss the stone from wherever it had been carried and catch it in the hands. In those days there were no sidewalks on which to draw the games with chalk, so they had to scratch them on the ground with a stick.

A hopscotch game we play now, with no tors and no numbers in the squares, is called LADDER. There can be ten squares, or fifteen, or any number you want, and it looks like this:

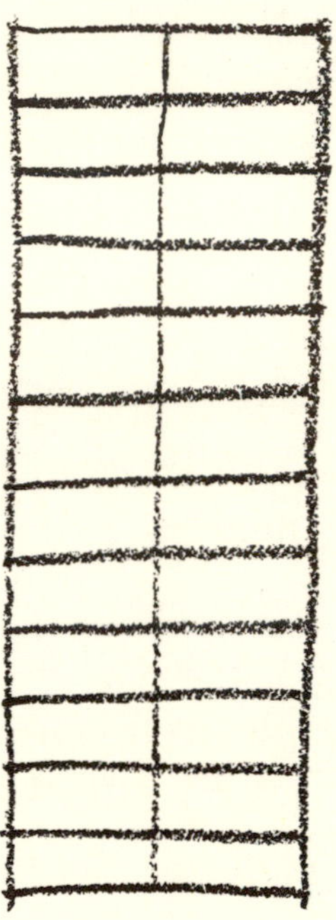

First you hop up and back, hopping in each square, and you can't put your other foot down even when you're turning around to come back. The next time you skip every other square. Then you skip two squares, and then three, and so on. It gets harder and harder. If you say at the beginning "no hands" then nobody can touch the ground with a hand for balance. Or you can say "no toesies" which means you can't put out a toe to touch the ground for balance. "No leg foot" means you can't balance even by throwing a leg to one side. The winner is the one who can skip the most number of squares without missing. Then you can play it all over again, using both feet, jumping instead of hopping.

In China, hopscotch is called T'AO FANG TZE. It's played on a long diagram divided into 8 or 10 squares. At the upper left there's a square called *Public House* where a player can rest on both feet. First throw your stone into 1, hop in, pick up your stone, throw it out, and hop out. Then throw your stone into 2, hop in 1, then 2, pick up your stone and throw it out, hop back to 1, then out. You can't touch a line or anyone's stone with your foot. Go through all the squares the same way. If you go through the whole game without a miss, you can mark off

a part of one square as your *Private House* and put your name in it. Then you can rest there, too, and no one else can hop in it or throw a stone in it. The one who gets the most private houses wins.

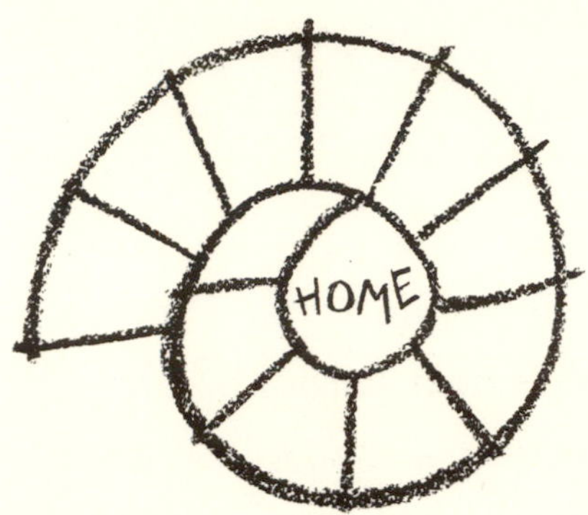

SNAIL is played the same as Ladder, first hopping in every square, then in every second square, then in every third one, and so on, only the place called *Home* is the beginning. First you start at the outside and hop into home. Then you hop out of home and around to the outside and back to home for the first part. It's like running away from home to get lost and then wanting to get unlost and back to home again.

The second game you do it on two feet, jumping.

WITCH is played on a Snail diagram. The one who is the witch is in the center, in her tower. The one who is the little girl or boy comes to the outside and knocks. The squares in the diagram are like steps in the long, curving stairway up to the witch's tower. When the child knocks, the witch calls down, "Just a minute, I'm putting on my girdle" (or hat, or whatever), then she goes down the steps and opens the door, and says, "What do you want?" The child says, "Ice cream" (or candy, or something like that). The witch says, "All right," and pulls the child upstairs. They can't step on a line even though they're both running. If they do, they fall downstairs. Finally they get to the top and the witch again asks, "What do you want?" and the child says, "Ice cream." Then the witch hollers, "Here's your ice cream!" and pushes the child out (off the top of the tower).

Next time the child is the witch and someone else is the child.

Another Snail kind of hopscotch has ten numbered squares and a home:

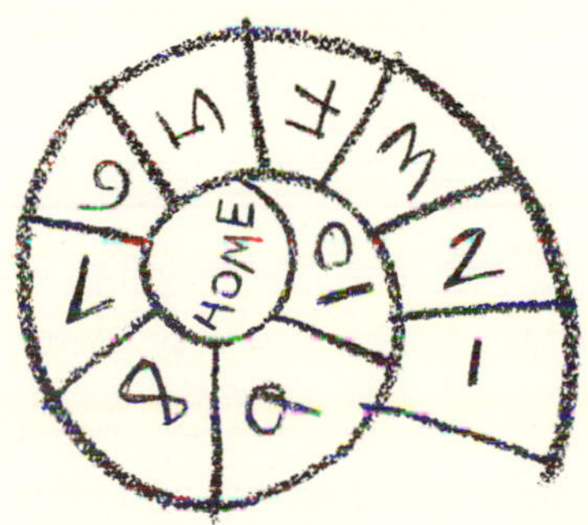

No tors are used. First you hop in each square up to home and back again. The next time you skip 1 and start in 2 and go around and back. Then you start in 3, and so on, leaving out another square at the beginning each time. At the very end all you do is hop into home and out again.

There are many different names for hopscotch. Some of them are: TRAY TRIP, BEDS, SCOTCH-BOB, HOP-BED, HOP-SCORE, HITCHIBED, PICKIE, and SCOTCHHOPPERS. In Scotland now it's called TEEVERS and there are three forms: PLAIN BEDS, FANCY BEDS, and FRENCH BEDS. In France it's called LA MARELLE and the tors are called *pions.*

SWAMP is a game that's not as easy as it looks:

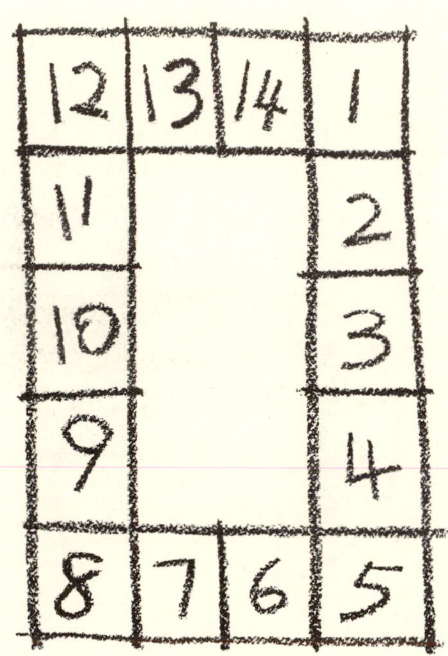

You start hopping at 1 and go around to 14. Then you have to hop backward, back to 1. The second time you use both feet and jump from 1 to 14, and then jump backward back to 1. It's hard when you have to do it backward. Of course you can't step on a line at all and you can't step in the middle, because the middle can be a swamp or a lake or any place terrible, as with crocodiles.

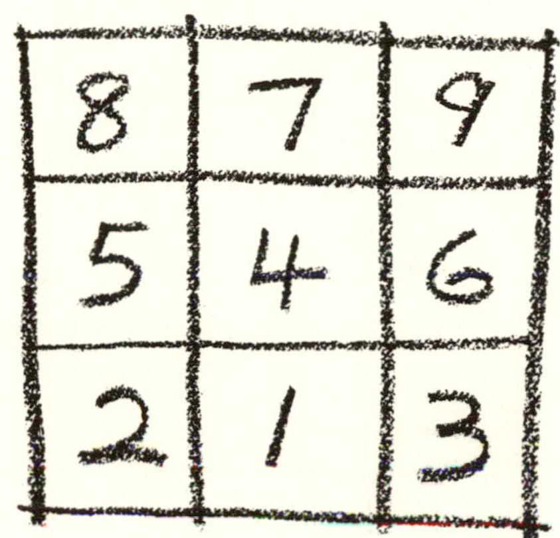

In 9-SQUARE hopscotch you jump, but sometimes the feet are together and sometimes they're apart. It's played without any numbers in the squares, but I have put numbers in the drawing so as to explain better how to do it. First both feet go into 1, then one foot goes into 2 while the other goes into 3. Then both are in 1 again, and then out. Next you jump to 4, then the left foot goes to 5 while the right foot goes to 6. Then both in 4, then both in 1, then 2-3, then 1 and out. Next you jump all the way to 7. Then your left foot goes in 8 while your right foot goes in 9. Then back to 7, then 4, next 5-6, 4, 1, 2-3, 1 and out.

Next you hop 1, 4, 5, and do the whole thing over again from that side. When you're through you hop 5,

4, 7 and so on until you've hopped the game from each side of the square. Then if you want to go on, you can do it from each corner, like this: 2, 5-1, 2 and out. 4, 8-3 (that's hard), 4, 2, 5-1, 2 and out. 9, 7-6, 9, 4, 8-3, 4, 2, 5-1, 2 and out. Then you can hop 2, 4, 8, and do it from the next corner and so on around the square again.

If you want to go on with the game after that, you can do it on two feet. First you jump into 1, then with both feet into 2, then to 3, then 1 and out. Next 4, then 5, then 6, 4, 1, 2, 3, 1, and out, and so on. But when you get to the second part, from the corners, it's always with the feet separate, as in the first part, otherwise it's too hard.

In Russia today there's a hopscotch game played the very same way as 9-Square. It's called RED LIGHT, GREEN LIGHT. You do it just the same way except with your eyes closed. Whenever you want, you can ask, "red light, green light?" Red light means you've missed, that is you've jumped in the wrong square or stepped on a line or something like that. Green light means you haven't missed. You don't have to ask, though, because your friends are standing around, and whenever you miss, they call out "red light." Then you can open your eyes to see how you've missed. Then it's the next player's turn.

16	13	14	15
12	9	10	11
8	5	6	7
4	1	2	3

THE VILLAGE is very much like 9-Square. There are no numbers in the squares, but I have put them in to explain the game. The first part is jumped in the same order as the first part of 9-Square except that the feet are always in different squares. First the left foot jumps into 1 while the right foot jumps into 2. Then the left foot jumps to 4 and the right to 3. Next back to 1 and 2 and then out. Then to 5 and 6 and so on through the whole game, the same as 9-Square except that you don't do it from the corners, because you can't.

In the second part of The Village both your feet are together all of the time. First jump into 1 with both feet, then with both feet into 2, then to 3, then all the way to 4, then to 1 and out. Next to 5, then 6, 7, 8, 5, 1 and out. 9, 10, 11, 12, 9, 5, 1, out. 13, 14, 15, 16, 13, 9, 5, 1, out. When you have finished this part from all four sides of The Village you've won the game.

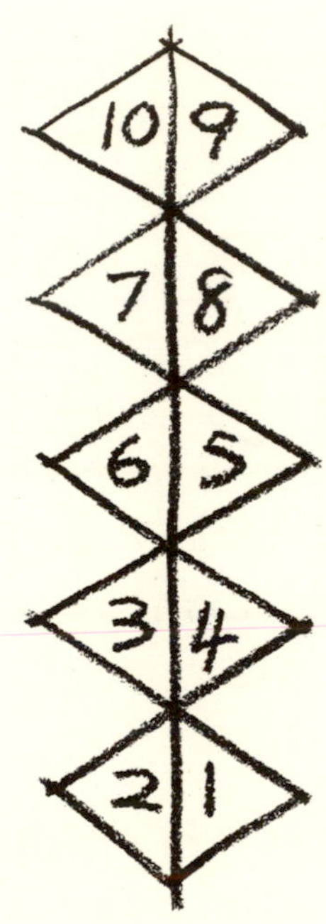

In playing TRIANGLES tors are used. You hop according to the numbers and don't step in a triangle where there's a tor. When you're hopping, say, from 3 to 4 or from 5 to 6 you hop sideways without turning toward the side. Otherwise it's like any long hopscotch.

Another kind of hopscotch with an unusual design is called MIX UP or MIX IT UP. It looks like this:

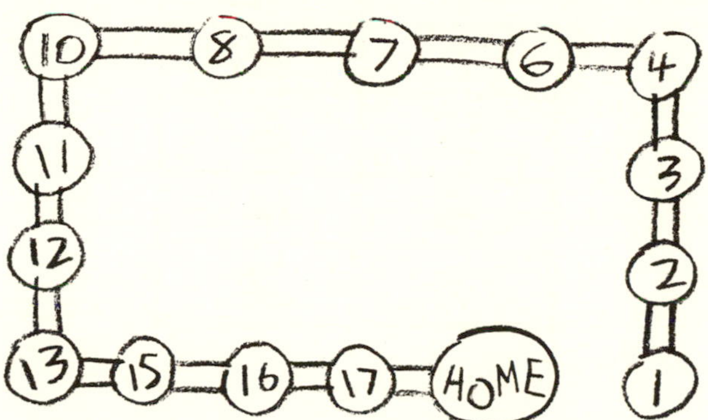

You will see that in three places numbers are skipped. You can put these anywhere in the game, but there can be only three of them. You hop around from 1 to home and then back to 1 again, but whenever you come to a place where the number is not in the right order, you have to skip that place. If you miss, it's the next player's turn and you have to start over. Whoever gets to home and back again first, wins.

There's another game on the same diagram, only the numbers are in the right order and tors are used. If there are three tors or maybe four in a row and you can't hop over them, you can say "butterscotch" and use one of the connecting links to step in.

Another hopscotch game played in Russia is drawn like this:

13	14
11	12
9	10
7	8
5	6
3	4
1	2

Throw your tor in 1 and hop 2, 4, 6, etc., around and back to 3. Pick up your tor and hop out. You can't ever step on a square you just picked up your tor from or a square where some other player's tor is. When you throw your tor in 2, you start hopping 1, 3, 5 and around that way. Each time you start hopping on the side your tor isn't on. Sometimes to make the game harder, you make a rule that everyone has to pick up the tor with the mouth instead of the hand.

When children play hopscotch in Burma, they squat down, sitting on their heels. To get from one square to the next, they give a sort of hop with both feet and land in the same squatting position. If you were to try this, you would find it very hard to do for a whole game.

There are many games to be played with pencils and paper that started out as hopscotch games. These are the different kinds of TIC TAC TOE like the one with nine squares in it where you put an O or X in one square each turn and try to get three in a row.

Then there's the one shaped like a pie cut into as many pieces as you want with a number in each piece. You shut your eyes and move your pencil around, saying, "Tic tac toe, around I go; where I stop I do not know." Then you put the point of your pencil down and if it goes into one of the parts of the game, that number is your score, and then it's the next person's turn. If your pencil point touches outside of the game your score is nothing. The winner is the first one to get a hundred points or a thousand, or whatever number you've decided will be the goal.

Another hopscotch on paper is the game LONDON where bits of paper are blown along a long diagram toward the goal. This is very similar to 11 POINTS which is a game we jump now. The diagram drawn on the sidewalk looks like this, but it can be as long as you want:

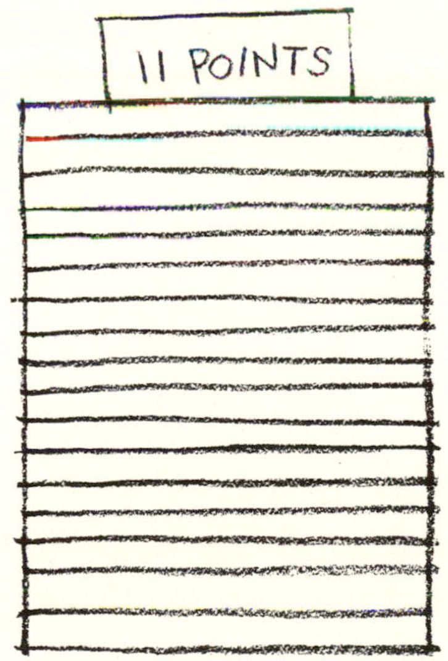

The first player jumps as far as he can, and puts his tor down where he lands, and then gets out of the way. Then the next player jumps from the beginning and puts his tor down where he lands, and so on until everyone has had a turn. Then the first one stands where his tor is and jumps again, and again puts his tor down to mark his place. When you get to the goal you have eleven points, and you start over at the beginning. The first one to get a hundred points is the winner. You're not supposed to run and jump, but jump from a standing position.

Another one that's fun is this:

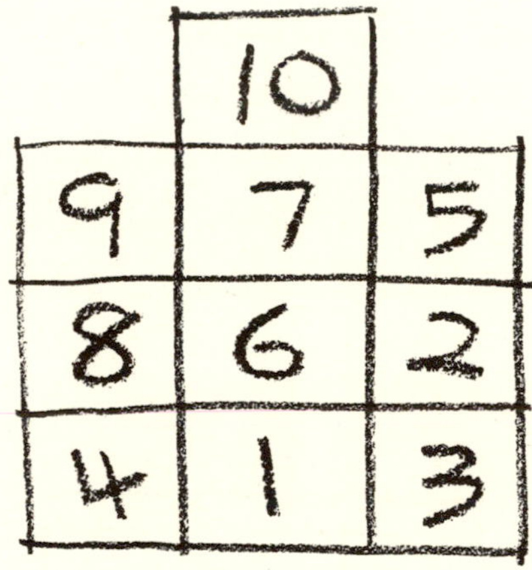

When you draw this one, you can put the numbers wherever you want, except 10 is always at the top. Then you hop *as fast as you can,* following the numbers in their right order no matter where they are. The second time through you jump on both feet. You have to be fast in this game and if you miss you have to start over.

The general way to play all the long hopscotch games is to use tors, hop in each square that's in a row, and jump with one foot into each of the squares that are side by side. You pick up your tor on the way back and throw it to the next number after you've gone through the game each time. A miss is to step on a line, step in a square where a tor is, or fail to throw your tor in the right square.

There are many kinds of long hopscotch and many, many rules for the different games. There are poison squares which you must avoid, or which are bad luck, sometimes for the other players. In this game:

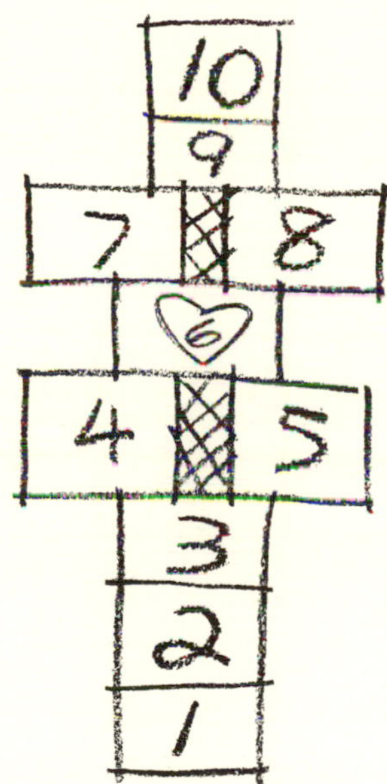

6 is poison and the places between 4 and 5 and between 7 and 8 are called *The Dragons.* If you step on one of the dragons you have to start again at 2. If, when you're

throwing for 6, your tor lands inside the heart, you can go to 9. And when you get to 4 and 5, if you can say "Jack and Jill" and turn around in one jump, before anyone else says it, you can start back without going on to 10!

Boxies are sometimes used in long hopscotch. They are boxes drawn alongside and connected to the diagram. If there are too many squares in a row with tors, you can hop to the boxie to help you get past them. Sometimes very little children use a boxie to throw their tor from to the higher numbers, when they can't throw as far as the other players.

In the following game the part marked H is for HEAVEN:

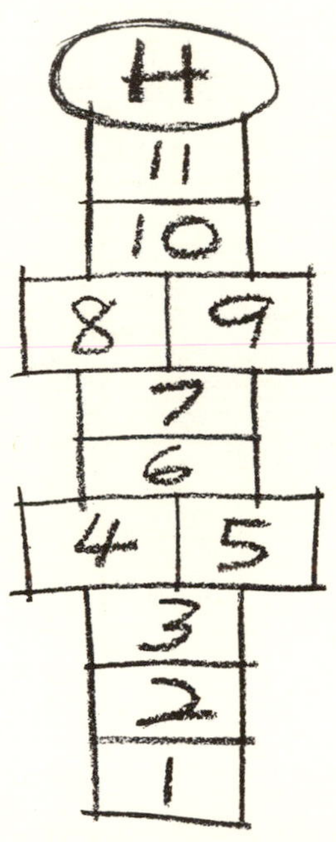

It is played in the usual way, except that when you are finishing the first part, on the way up, you throw your tor into Heaven. Then you hop to 11, pick up your tor, jump to the very spot where your tor landed in Heaven, and say, as fast as you can, the alphabet forward and backward, your name, address, and telephone number (if you have one), your age, and the name of your boy-friend or girl-friend (if you have one of those).

Sometimes the game called Heaven is drawn like this:

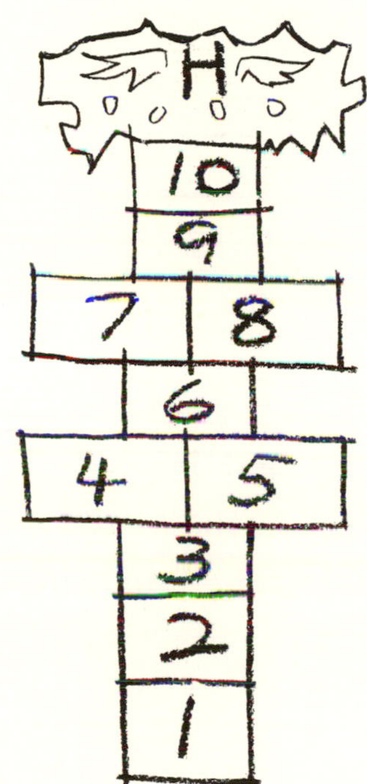

The Heaven part is shaped like a cloud and has the H in it, and also little wings and halos. But it's played like any long hopscotch.

Another long hopscotch is drawn like this:

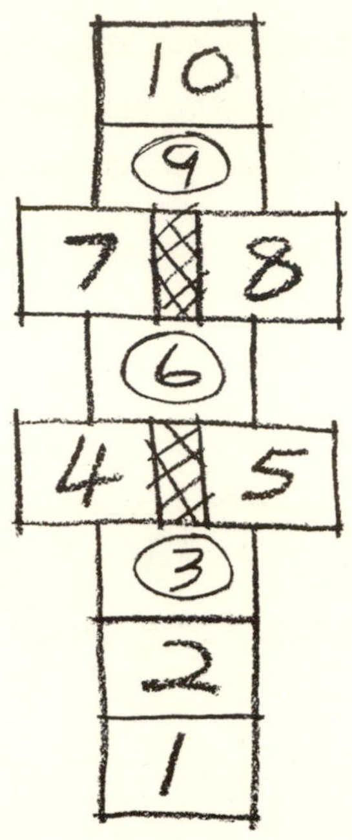

3, 6, and 9 are poison; usually you can't step in them but you do throw your tor in them. 1, 2, 4-5, 7-8 and 10 are the only squares you usually hop or jump into. Boxies are used when the distance is too long because of tors in the squares, or for the littler children to throw from.

When you are on your way up from 1 to 10, you pick up your tor on the way back, then you say "buttercups" and step in the square, even if it's a poison square. After you've gone to 10 on your way up, you have to stand beyond 10 and throw your tor to 1. If you miss, it's the next player's turn. You have to get in 1 before you start back. When you do you hop all the way back, even in the poison squares, get your tor, go back to 10 and start back, throwing the tor to 9, and so on, back to 1. The only difference is that you pick up your tor as you go up the numbers where before you picked it up as you came back. But you have to pay attention to the poison squares as in the first part.

In another game played on the same diagram, you throw your tor in 1, hop to 2, then jump so your left foot goes in 4 while your right foot goes in 5. Then you say "Jack and Jill" as you jump so that your feet land in the opposite squares and you're facing 1 again. Hop to 2 and then out. Then you go to 2, 4-5, 7-8, Jack and Jill twice, to 10 and out at that end. Next you hop to 10, jump to 7-8, say "Jack and Jill," go back to 10, and then come all the way back to 2, pick up your tor, hop to 1 and out. You have to do this each time you go up the game. The game is finished when you've gone through 10; you don't have to come back with your tor.

Sometimes in long hopscotch when there are poison squares, you can make a rule called CLICK AND CLAP. Click is clicking your heels together, and Clap is clapping your hands. If there is one tor in a poison square that you have to hop over, you have to click while you're hopping and also say the word. If there are two or more tors you must click and clap, and say it, all in one hop. You do this only when going over poison squares.

But not all long games have poison squares and special words. The following one has none of these and is probably the most usual of all hopscotch games:

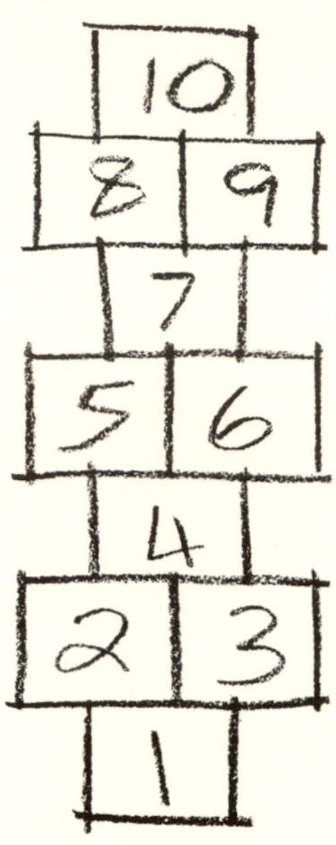

First throw your tor to 1, jump over it so your left foot is in 2 and your right foot in 3. Hop to 4, jump 5-6, hop 7, jump 8-9, hop 10 and out. Come back the same way, stooping to pick up your tor, then hop in 1 and out. Then throw your tor to 2, hop 1, 3, 4, jump 5-6, and so on. Keep on until you miss, when it's the next player's turn. Whenever anyone steps on a line or in a square with a tor it's a miss.

The next game is hopped just the same as the last one on the way up to 12. Then when you're through

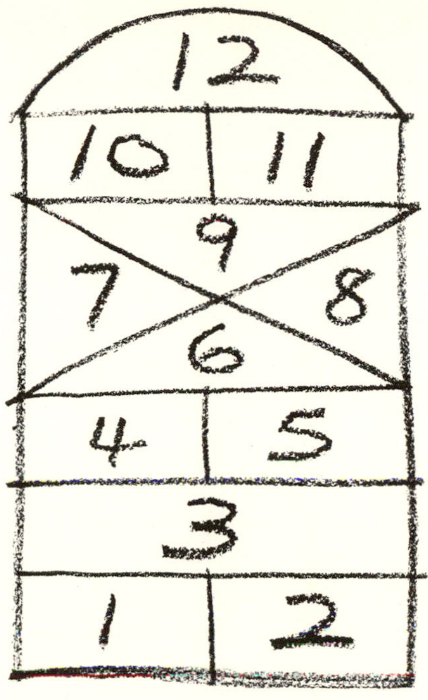

with that, throw your tor past 12, hop up to where your tor landed, pick it up, and throw it to 12. Hop back to 11 and back to 1 and then up again. Pick up your tor when you get to 11, hop to 12 and out. Then throw it to 11. Go through the whole game on the way back to 1 in the same way. If you get back to 1 first, you've won the game.

These long games with the rounded ends originally were supposed to represent the dome of a church, later the dome of Heaven, and, much later, a pudding. There's an old English hopscotch that's called ONESIE, TWOSIE, THREESIE, FOURSIE, PUDDINGS. Sometimes now instead of an H in the last square a pudding is drawn.

Another one looks like this:

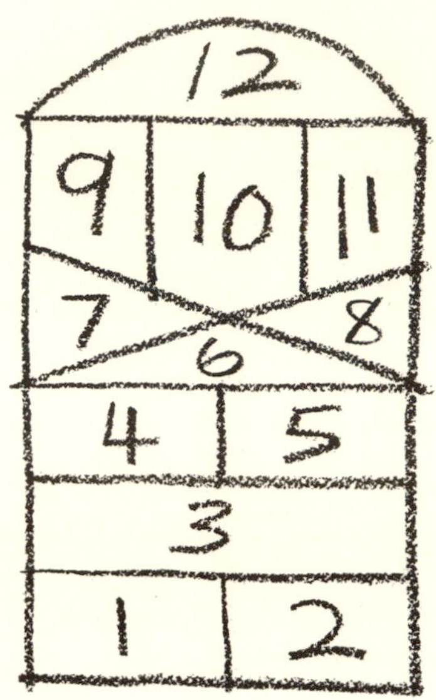

It's played the same way as the last one, except you go 1-2, 4-5, 7-8, 9-11, 12. Of course if there's a tor in 1, you hop 2, then jump 4-5, and so on. 3, 6 and 10 are poison. You have to throw your tor into them but you don't hop in them.

GAREEKA is a hopscotch game which started in Russia and is now played in this country as well.

First you throw your tor into onesies and then hop 2, 3, 4, 5, 6, 7, 13, 11, 9. Lean over and pick up your tor and hop out. Then throw it into twosies, and hop 3,

4, 5, 6, 7, 12, 10, 8. Pick up your tor and hop out. You come back on a different side each time.

Each time you throw your tor into the next number, you can't hop in any of the lower numbers: when you throw your tor into fivesies, your first hop should be to sixies. But of course that's too far so you use 9 and 11 and 13 as boxies, or 8, 10, and 12. Then you hop to 7, then 6, pick up your tor, and hop back 5, 4, 3, 2, 1, and out.

When you throw your tor into 8, hop 9, 11, 13, 12, 10, pick up your tor, 8, and out. When you throw your tor to 9 your hopping starts at 8. For the last six squares you always start hopping on the side that your tor isn't on.

A tor is used in this game, and of course you can't hop in any square where there is a tor. And you lose your turn if you throw your tor so that it rests on any line. You can rest with one foot in 4 and one foot in 5, both hopping up and hopping back, but that is the only place you can rest; at 10 you must turn around just on your one hopping foot.

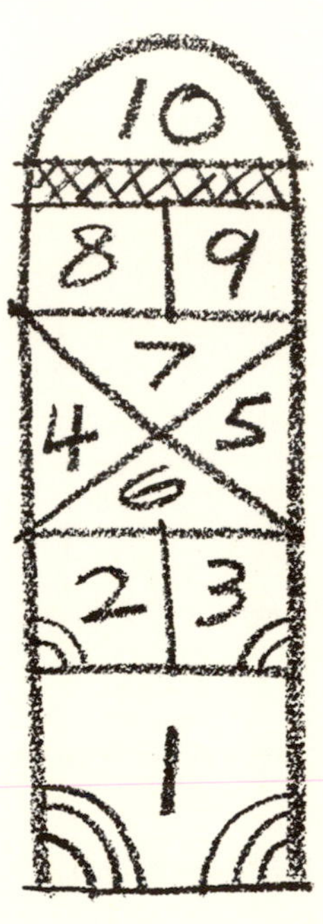

Book Three

WHO'S IT?

Put down your basket
And play with me.
Who will be it?
We'll count and see.

The person who has to be IT is the one who has to take the leading part in the game to be played. Sometimes it's more fun not to be IT, but some people would rather be IT all of the time.

There are many ways of finding out who's IT. Sometimes the first person to speak up can be IT. Another way is for everyone playing to stand in a circle, with one person in the middle. That one shuts his eyes and turns around five times, or three times, then stops and points to the one who's IT. Or a race can be run and the last one in is IT. Sometimes a ring is drawn on the ground and everyone stands inside of it and then at a given signal they all try to step outside of it at once. The last one out is IT.

Drawing straws or tossing a coin or asking "which hand do you want" are other ways.

But rhymes for counting-out are the most fun. This is the oldest way to find out who's IT. It's like casting lots to find out who is to be the victim.

The one who is IT is the one who is *hit,* struck, touched for doom. It is the tabooed one, the unnamed one, the IT, the ritualistic victim.

Sometimes these rhymes sound like magic incantations. Some of them may have been. Others can be traced to counting one, two, three, and so on, in other, older languages.

But the verses change. New words are added because they make a rhyme or because the sound is similar to a forgotten word in the verse.

All of the rhymes in this collection are in use now in this country, but some of them can be traced back for hundreds of years. A few variations of the same rhymes are given here because it is interesting to see how they can change.

Counting-out rhymes are so old that we will never know when or where they were first used. But they are also as new as today because anyone can make them up.

It used to be that each game had its own special counting-out rhyme. Now any rhyme can be used for any game.

Who's IT?

Judy's IT
And got a fit
And don't know how
To get out of it!

Usually when counting-out, everyone stands in a circle and the player who is doing the counting points to each person in turn, including himself, as he says the rhyme, tapping or pointing to each one in rhythm to the rhyme. When the verse is finished the last one pointed to is out and the rhyme is started again. The last person left in the circle is IT. Sometimes this turns out to be the one who is doing the counting!

In some of the rhymes, you stick both of your fists out in front of you and the counter-out taps each fist. When he comes to himself he taps his nose in place of the hand he's using to do the tapping, and then his other fist. The last hand touched is placed behind the player's back and the rhyme is said again. This is continued until the one who is IT is discovered, either because he's the first one to have both hands tapped, or because he's the last one.

Some players say a rhyme only once, and the person pointed to at the last word of the rhyme is the one who has to be IT.

During some other rhymes the feet are pointed to instead of the players themselves or their hands. Each player puts one foot in the circle and takes it out when his foot is "out." The one with his foot left in at the end is IT.

You don't point to a different person with each word or each syllable. You point around with the beat of the rhythm of the rhyme.

Sometimes these rhymes are used to find out who's IT just for the fun of it even when you aren't going to play a game.

Intry mintry cutry corn
Apple seed and apple thorn
Wire, brier, limberlock.
Three geese in a flock
One flew east
And one flew west
And one flew over the the cuckoo's nest.

Eeney meeney
Mink munk
Klink klunk
Ooza vooza
Veckidee
Eish feish
Feck.

Eeny meeny miney mo
Catch a tiger by the toe
If he hollers let him go
Eeny meeny miney mo.

or:

If he hollers make him pay
Fifty dollars every day.

Eeny meenie
Dixie deeny
Skinamacracker
Tom and Neeny
Ein swein
Bumble bein
Eighteen hundred and ninety-nine.

Eenie meenie tipsy teenie
Apple Jack Paul Sweeney
Dotchy potchy Don Morotchy
O, par, dar, see
Out goes Y-O-U.

1, 2, 3,
Rover got a flea.
4, 5, 6,
Rover got a tick.
7, 8, 9,
He wants a glass of wine.

1, 2, 3, 4, 5, 6, 7,
All good children go to Heaven.
When they get there they will say
Johnny, oh Johnny went the other way.

W. P. A., W. P. A.
You're let out
Go get your pay.

A
E
I
O
U! *(you)*

Ibbady bibbady sibbady sab
Ibbady bibbady kanolla
Kanolla in
Kanolla out
Kanolla over the water spout.

Ibbety bibbety sibbety sab
Ibbety bibbety canal boat
Dictionary
Down the ferry
Out goes Y O U.

Ibbety bibbety sibbety sab
Ibbety bibbety conago
Uska buska nom and uska
Hi pan lo
Out you go.

Ibbety bibbety sibbety Sam
Ibbety bibbety canal canoe
Up the river, down the river
Out goes Y O U.

My mother your mother
was hanging out clothes
My mother gave your mother
a punch in the nose
Did it hurt?
Say yes or no.
Y E S spells yes
And out you go.

Onerie ory ickerie Ann
Fillisie follisie Nicholas John
Queevum quorum Irish Mary
Stinkelum stunkelum
Buck.

Monry orey ickery Ann
Philisy pholosy Nicholas John
Queevy, quavy, English Navy
Stinkem, stankem, buck.

One's all, two's all, zig a zall zan
Bobtail nanny goat, tittle tall tan
Harum scarum merchant marun
Sinctum sanctum
Buck.

Onery twoery zickery zan
Hollowbone crackabone ninery ten
Spit spot it must be done
Twiddelum twaddelum twenty-one.

Eena deena dina dust
Cattle weela wila wust
Spin spun must be done
Twiddelum twaddelum twenty-one
O U T spells out.

Butter, leve, bone, stry
Hair, brit, brof, nack
We, wo, wack
O U T spells
Out goes he.

Cricky cracky craney crow
I went to the well to wash my toe
High and low
Out you go
Cricky cracky craney crow.

Ishka biska tiska too
Once around and out goes you.

1, 2, 3, 4, 5, 6, 7
All good children go to heaven
1, 2, 3, 4, 5, 6, 7, 8
All bad children have to wait.

1, 2, 3, 4, 5, 6, 7
All good children go to heaven
Penny on the water
Two cents on the sea
Three cents on the railroad
Out goes she.

1, 2, 3, 4
Mary at the cottage door
5, 6, 7, 8
Eating cherries off a plate
O U T spells out.

1, 2, 3, 4
Mama scrub the kitchen floor
Floor dried
Baby cried
1, 2, 3, 4.

1, 2, 3 a nation
I received my confirmation
On the day of declaration
1, 2, 3 a nation.

One two three
The bumblebee
The rooster crows
Out goes she.

Impty dimpty tibbity fig
Delia dauma nauma nig
Heitcha peitcha
Dauma neitcha
Ein pine pug
Ullaga bullaga boo
*Out goes YO*U.

Ella mella deek ortella
Shebegora ootbahora
Riggy run
Toogy spun
Snip snap
Snoota oota.

Engine, engine number nine
Running on Chicago line
If she's polished
How she'll shine!
Engine, engine number nine.

Engine engine
Number nine
Running down
Chicago line
See her sparkle
See her shine
Engine engine
Number nine.

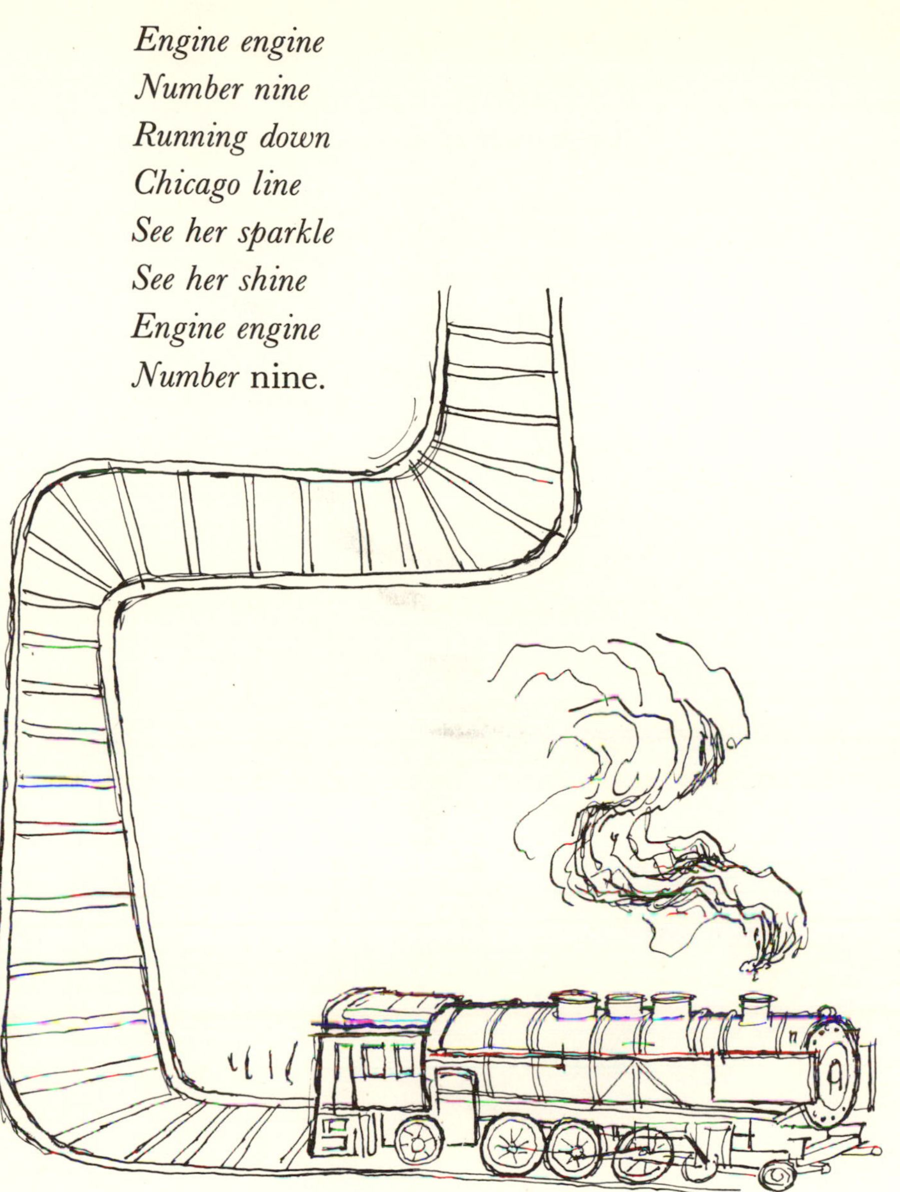

Engine engine number nine
I am silver, I am fine.
When I stare along the track
People stand and stare right back.

Fun, fun
Son of a gun
Eighteen hundred and ninety-one.

Ish nee sunk
She go roo
Kish kosh koo
Ju ju-ju.

E do me do
So fa la la
Ecka pisha tal
And a jingaso ta
Watermelons, watermelons
A nickel for two
Out goes you.

All the monkeys at the zoo
Had their tails painted blue
One two three
Out goes you.

Tit tat toe
Round I go.
If I miss
I just take this.

Looby Lou
Looby Lou
When I'm finished
Out goes you.

Little sinner
Come to dinner
Half past two
Fried potatoes
Alligators
Out goes you.

In the following rhymes the last person pointed to answers the question with one word. Then the counter-out spells that word around the circle.

Your mother and my mother
Were hanging out clothes
Your mother gave my mother
A punch in the nose.
What color did it run?

If answer is "red," for example, the counter-out then spells R E D, tapping whoever comes to be IT on D.

or:

Did it hurt?

My doggie died last night
What color was his blood?

The sky is blue.
How old are you?

Mickey Mouse made a house.
How many bricks did he use?

This next one is like this: One person turns his back and another tiptoes up behind him and says the rhyme in a funny voice while making a circle around and around on his back with one finger. At the word "in" he pokes his finger in the other person's back. If the one whose back is turned can guess who did it, then the one who did it is IT. If he can't guess then he is IT.

A riddle
A diddle
A hole in the middle
Somebody stuck
His finger in.

These are rhymes for counting-out where your feet are the things you point to.

Eeny meeny
Miney mo
This foot
Got to go.

Doggie, doggie
Step
right
out.

Too many horses
In the stable.
One steps out.

And in these your fists are used.

One potato
Two potatoes
Three potatoes
Four
Five potatoes
Six potatoes
Seven potatoes
More.

One a penny
Two a penny
Three a penny
Four
Five a penny
Six a penny
Seven a penny
More.

One of the following is sometimes added to the end of any rhyme.

Oh you old dirty dishrag
You go out.

With a dirty dishrag
Turned inside out
And over the deep blue sea.

Sit and sing
By a spring
O U T
And in again.

My mother said
For me to pick
The very best
One.

Book Four

JACKS

In the springtime when boys start flying their kites and playing marbles, the girls get out their jacks and balls and start playing *JACKS.* In winter when it's cold and wet outside, jacks are fun indoors.

When we play jacks now we use ten metal jacks like this:

and a small rubber ball:

Nobody knows when people first started to play jacks, but we do know they used other things to play with: little bones like knuckle bones, or stones or shells or little pottery pieces . . . and they didn't even have a ball. They'd use one of the pieces to throw up and catch, with no bouncing.

Some people say that the ancient Romans were the first to play jacks because there are statues of them doing it. The game was called *Tali.* There are also pictures of people playing jacks on ancient Greek vases. But some people think that everything started in Greece or Rome, and this is not always so.

Jacks are played by people all over the world that the Romans never visited. The Piute Indians here in the United States played a game like jacks with rocks as big as your fist, piled up like this:

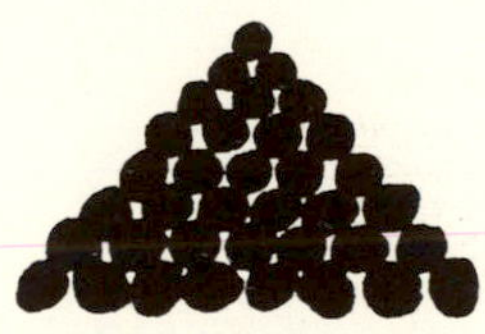

They'd toss up another rock of the same size, pick a rock from the pile and catch the tossed rock in the same hand. If they didn't miss they could keep the rock from the pile and pass the tossing rock on to the next person. The one with the most rocks at the end won.

A traveler through Russia in 1810 wrote that the people played jacks all through that country, using the little joint bones of sheep.

When you start a game of jacks, the first thing to do is to sit down on the floor, take the jacks in your hands, and Pinkie. To pinkie is to throw the jacks up, catch them on the back of your hand, throw them from there, and catch them in your palm. Some people use both hands for this and some use only one. The jacks that drop on the floor are the ones you start playing the game with. The jacks that haven't dropped are kept in your left hand while you go through Onesies.

Sometimes a rule is made that if you don't drop any jacks when you first pinkie, so that you would start on Twosies, you can pinkie again instead of doing Twosies, and if you don't drop any you can pinkie again for Threesies, and so on up the games.

To play ONESIES, pick up the ball, toss it up, pick up a jack with the same hand, and catch the ball after it has bounced once. Repeat this, using only one hand, picking up the other jacks one by one. In any game of jacks, when you pick up the jacks one by one, it's called "Onesies." When you have finished this, if you haven't made a miss, you can go on to TWOSIES, which is the same thing except that after throwing all the jacks out, you pick them up two by two.

Sometimes the rule is that all of the jacks have to be kept in your right hand as you go through Onesies, Twosies, or whatever part of the game you're on. Most people play that when the ball is tossed up, you pick up the jack and then catch the ball, and then you can put the jack in your left hand, before you toss the ball again.

To miss is very easy. It can be if you touch or move a jack you're not picking up. Or if you miss the ball. Or if the ball lands on a jack, then you have to say "split-jack" before anyone else says it, and it's a miss if you can't do this and catch the ball, too. Some players have it that if the ball lands on a jack, you have to say "pop-a-jack" or just "pop-jack," but if this happens twice in any one game it's a miss no matter what you say. A miss is also called an "out." Or a miss can be if you drop the ball or any jack when you're not supposed to. And you can't hit another player with a jack when you're throwing out the jacks, or that player can put the jack where she wants.

For THREESIES you pick up three jacks, then three more, then three more, and then the one that's left over. In FOURSIES it's four, four, then two.

Some people play that if the jacks are in a difficult arrangement and it would be easier, say in foursies, to pick up two, then four and then the other four, you can say "carts before horses" and do it that way, but usually you can't and CARTS BEFORE HORSES is a separate game. And some play that you have to pinkie before Twosies, Threesies, and so on and that if you drop more jacks than the game you're on it's a miss. Very few people play this way.

In FIVESIES you pick up five and then five. In SIXIES it's six and then four, and so on up through TENSIES. After you get through Tensies, that's the end of the first game. Tensies is also called ALLSIES. And when you throw the jacks out for Tensies, the spread of the jacks has to be bigger than the spread of your hand, otherwise you can't pick them up and it's a miss.

In the eastern part of this country BACKSIES is played by some people after each game, and you're not through with a game until you've played it. To play Backsies, you throw all the jacks down, toss the ball up and pick up all the jacks, catching the ball on the first bounce. Throw the jacks out again, and pick them all up except one. Throw out the nine you have in your hand, and pick them all up except two, of course bouncing the ball each time you pick up the jacks. Continue like this until there are none left to pick up. The ones that are left on the floor always have to be the same ones.

There is a great difference of opinion as to which game of jacks is the *second* game to play, and the *third* and so on. So the order I give you the games in can be changed if you want to.

The second game is called CHERRIES IN THE BASKET and is played just the same as the first game except that when you pick up the jacks you have to put them in your left hand *before* catching the ball each time.

And then you play Backsies again if you're playing that way. Backsies is always played the same way no matter what game you're on.

When you throw out the jacks in any game, you have to stay in the same place to play. Even if it looks easier from the other side, you can't move around to there.

But sometimes you're in a tight spot and then you're just bound to miss.

And when you throw them out, what if one jack lands on top of another? Well, you can call out "haystacks" or "kings" before anyone else does, and then you can pick up the top one and put it anywhere you want to, to make it easy. But if another player says it first, then that player can pick up both jacks, and say "bombs away" and drop them from as high as she can reach, but still sitting down, which usually makes them fall so far that the game is very hard. Another way is if you throw the jacks and one lands on top of another you have to pick up the two jacks, kiss them, and toss them out again. Or you just say "kisses," because one is on top of the other, but you don't really do it, and then you toss those two again. Some people call two jacks close together side by side, like this:

a kiss.

The third game is PIGS IN THE PEN. You hold your left hand on the floor with the little-finger side of it and all of your thumb down, and all of the fingertips together and down. The thumb is stretched away, and between the thumb and the first finger is arched up so there's a space under the palm of your left hand for the jacks to be put. You go through the game from Onesies to Tensies, only you don't pick up the jacks. You toss up the ball, push one of the "pigs" into the "pen," and catch the ball after the first bounce. The pigs in this game are the jacks, and the pen is your left hand. On Twosies, you push the pigs into the pen two by two, and so on.

Another game, that I don't know the name of, has a rhyme that you say as you play it. It goes like this:

Sweep the floor
Move the chair
Pick it up
And put it there.

You pinkie, as you do before all new games. Then when you start to play you toss up the ball, rub your fingertips over the floor, and catch the ball. On the next toss of the ball you pick up a jack and move it a short way, and then catch the ball. Next toss you pick up the same jack and put it out of the way. Then catch the ball. Going through this with each jack from Onesies to Tensies can become quite tiresome.

HESITATION is another game. After you pinkie, you play it like this: Toss the ball up, pick up a jack, catch the ball on the first bounce. Toss the ball up again, put the jack in your other hand, and catch the ball after one bounce. Continue in this way from Onesies through Tensies.

In another game which is similar but faster, you throw the ball, pick up a jack, and catch the ball. Throw the ball again and then put the jack in your other hand

and pick up the next jack before you catch the ball again on the first bounce. When you get to the end of Onesies and you have one jack in your hand and no more to pick up, you toss the ball, transfer the last jack to the other hand, and then slap the floor before you catch the ball. Some people play that at the end of Twosies you slap the floor twice, and at the end of Threesies you slap the floor three times and so on, but this is almost impossible when you get up near Tensies.

OVER THE FENCE, or HORSES OVER THE FENCE, is another game. For this you hold your left hand with the little-finger side of it down on the floor and the rest of it up so as to make a fence. As you toss the ball and pick up each jack, you put the jacks over the fence—that is, on the floor on the other side of your left hand—before you catch the ball on the first bounce each time. When all the "horses" are over the "fence" you move your left hand away, toss the ball, and pick up all ten at once, and then catch the ball again. Then you go on to Twosies, when the horses have to go over the fence two by two. And so on up through Tensies.

This is very much like an old English game called CHUCKS that was played with five small stones. As you lifted them one by one you had to say this rhyme:

Sweep the floor
Lift a chair
Sweep below it
And lay it down.
Cream the milk
Cream the milk
Quick, quick, quick
Spread a piece of butter on it
Thick, thick, thick.

In AROUND THE WORLD you toss up the ball and pick up a jack. Then you have to wave your hand over the ball and around and under it before you catch it. Then you put the jack in your other hand.

In any of these games it's a miss if the ball doesn't bounce exactly once, unless you're playing No-Bounce or Double-Bounce or Triple-Bounce.

In NO-BOUNCE you play just as in the first game except that when you toss the ball up, you have to pick up a jack and catch it on the way down and it never touches the floor at all. This is a very fast game and lots of fun if you can do it. In DOUBLE-BOUNCE the ball bounces twice each time instead of once, and in TRIPLE-BOUNCE it bounces three times. You have to have a pretty good ball for these last two and you have to throw it a little higher than usual.

SHOOTING STARS is a very pretty game. You toss your ball up and pick up a jack and then catch the ball. On the next bounce of the ball you toss the jack from your right hand and catch it in your left hand while you pick up the next jack and catch the ball with your right hand. If your jacks are bright and shiny, this is almost as pretty to watch as it is fun to play.

Jacks is a game that is played all over the world because the things to play it with are available anywhere. Many different things can be, and are, used. Cherry stones are good, or plum stones. And many people use just these, with no ball. One of the cherry stones is thrown up instead of a ball. Of course then it's always no-bounce.

In the Phillippines the game is called SONCA. In India it's called GUTTAK. In China the game is called CATCHING SEVEN PIECES. There they use seven little cloth bags about one inch square. The bags are filled with sand and then sewed up all around the edges:

In France today they still play it with knucklebones, which was an older name for the game in England. They called it KNUCKLEBONES or sometimes HUCKLEBONES. ASHUKH is the name given to the game in Persia. It is pronounced "Ow-shoock." And they use knucklebones, too, usually from sheep, but the game is more like the way we play marbles than it is like jacks.

In Bolivia a kind of combination game is played with one marble for tossing, and five little stones.

Jackstones have been found in Ireland in a special hole beside the fireplaces in ancient crannogs. A crannog is a house built in the middle of a lake. This keeps unwelcome visitors away.

In Japan the game of jacks is called TEDAMA.

The origin of the game is probably Asiatic. The pastern-bones of sheep, goats, or calves were used. Each of these bones had two rounded ends, two broad sides and two narrow sides, one of each of the latter two pairs being concave and the other convex. Each side had a different score to it. So this is like the beginnings of games using dice. Then when they were played with and tossed into holes in the ground, it's like the beginnings of the game of marbles. When these became three separate games, jacks was still played with only five pieces. Later still we played it with ten to make it more fun.

Different names for jacks are: KNUCKLEBONES, HUCKLEBONES, DIBS, JACKSTONES ("jack" meaning "little"), CHUCKSTONES ("chuck" means to throw something a short distance), and FIVE-STONES. This was played by tossing one up and catching it on the back of the hand, and then on the palm of the same hand. Then tossing up two and catching them on the back of the hand and then on the palm. And then three, and so on up to five. This is still fun to play with pebbles or with real jacks. And it's a good way to learn how to pinkie.

CHECKSTONES was played with five cubes about a half inch in diameter and a ball. All of these were made of pottery. CHUCKS was played with a kind of shell or with pebbles, and in Scotland was called CHUCKIE-STANES. DABS and SNOBS are other names for the game, where one stone was tossed up and caught and no ball was used. DIBS was played with little bones.

One old game that's fun is CRADLE: you arrange the jacks to look like a cradle:

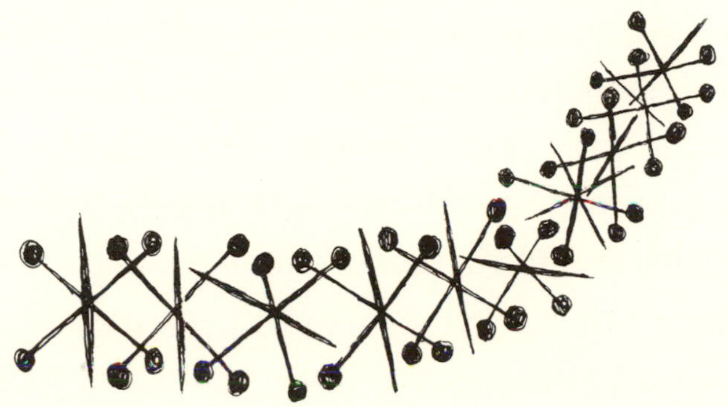

Then you bounce the ball and pick them up one at a time, *without* disturbing any of the other jacks. This one takes some practice, but once you can do it, you can do something that few other players can.

Another that's similar is called CHIMNEY. The jacks are piled up one on another.

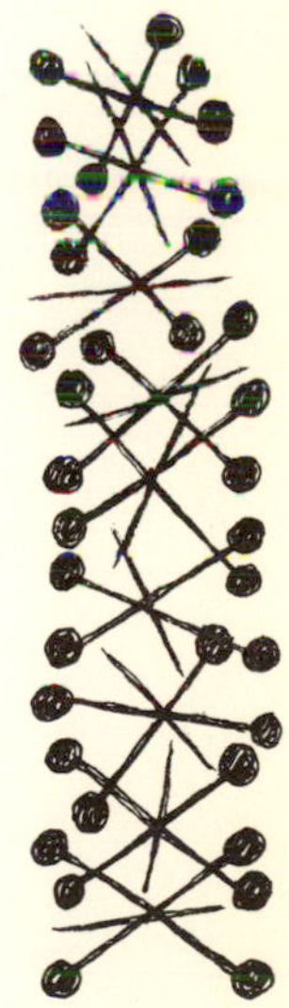

When you bounce the ball the first time you take off the top jack. After you catch the ball, you put the jack in your other hand. Then you do the same, taking off the second jack, and so on. Of course you can't topple down the chimney while you're playing this! I've seen lots of people try to do this game, but I've never seen anyone able to. And I don't really think it's possible unless maybe your jacks are perfectly made and balanced.

In England a long time ago the different games of jacks were played in this order: BABY GAME, DOWNS AND UPS, EGGS IN BASKET, CRACK THE EGGS, UPCAST, DOWNCAST, PIGS IN THE PEN, SWEEPS, SCRUBS, DOUBLE BOUNCE, BOUNCE NO-BOUNCE. Some of these games we don't even know any more. And there is a great deal of difference about the order in which we play the various games we know. Some people play that after the second game, you can play any one you want. The first player to get to the beginning of the third game can call out "followsies," and then the other players have to play their third game the same as that player, as in Follow the Leader. Then if another player finishes the third game before everyone else, she can call out "followsies" and choose the fourth game.

One game that some players use for the third game is called DOWN BOUNCE. It's played just like regular jacks only instead of tossing the ball up, you throw it down. Then you pick up a jack, and catch the ball before it bounces again.

Very little children and beginning players have something they call OVERS or OVERSIES. When they throw down the jacks and they land in a way that's going to be hard to play, they quickly pick up the jacks again and say "overs" or "oversies" and throw them out again.

JACKYSTEAUNS is one old name for the game, and so is CHACKSTONES. It sounds almost like our word Jackstones.

Another modern game is played this way: after the jacks have been pinkied, you toss up the ball, pick up a jack, and put it aside and catch the ball. Repeat this until all the jacks are arranged in a line, with enough space in between for your thumb to fit. Then toss up the ball again and catch it on the back of your hand. To do this you must have your first and third fingers slightly raised and your middle finger slightly down. Now, with the ball on the back of your hand, you run your thumb of the same hand in and out between the jacks, like a grapevine, up the row and back again without dropping the ball. Then you toss up the ball from the back of your hand, pick up all the jacks at once, and catch the ball.

When you're on Twosies you arrange the jacks two by two in the row. When you get to Ninesies it's just like a figure-eight sign that you make with your thumb around the jacks. And when you're on Tensies, you go around the pile three times with your thumb.

One game that's lots of fun if you're fast enough is the one in which you pick up one jack at a time only. Onesies is played just like ordinary jacks, but when you're on Twosies you toss up the ball and pick up one jack and then another before you catch the ball. On Threesies you pick up one and then another and then the third before catching the ball, and so on. Nobody gets very far in this game.

For this next game you have to hold your left hand palm down on the floor, with the fingers spread wide apart and pointing toward the jacks. Of course you pinkie first, then hold your left hand down as explained. As you toss up the ball you shove one of the jacks between your little finger and the next one of your left hand, and catch the ball. On the next toss the next jack goes between the next fingers, and so on until all the jacks are between the various fingers of your left hand, and maybe you have three or four jacks between each finger.

Then you toss up the ball, pick up your left hand full of jacks and transfer all the jacks to your other hand before you catch the ball. Then you're ready to start Twosies, if you haven't made a miss. In Twosies you shove the jacks between your fingers two by two.

CHINESE JACKS is another game we play in this country. I think it's just called that and doesn't really have anything to do with China. It's one of the few games in which you don't pinkie at the beginning. You throw out the jacks and toss up your ball and pick up one jack and then catch the ball. Then you transfer the jack to your other hand. On the next toss of the ball you pick up two jacks. On the third toss, three jacks, and on the fourth toss, four. Then you throw the jacks out again, and on the first toss of the ball you pick

up four jacks, catch the ball, and put the jacks in your other hand. Then toss the ball and pick up three jacks and catch the ball and put the jacks in your other hand. And so on, with two and then one jack. Then the game is over. It's a very short game, but it's fun.

When you play BROADWAY you have to sit near a wall. The wall can be anything, even another player's leg. After you pinkie, you roll the ball toward the wall, pick up a jack, and then pick up the ball before it touches the wall. After you go through Onesies, and you're on

Twosies, you roll the ball toward the wall and pick up the jacks two by two, each time catching the ball before it hits the wall. You see, there's no bouncing in this one, just the ball rolling along. It's cheating if you roll the ball so slowly that it never would reach the wall.

There are lots of different games given here, but when you have a real tournament or contest you play only the first game, over and over, and it's kind of like a spelling bee. Different players drop out because they've missed until only one is left and then she's the champion.

Often when you're playing like this you don't pinkie but you throw out the jacks and throw up the ball from the same hand at the same time, and start playing immediately. When you throw the jacks out that is called scrambling, and the arrangement of jacks on the floor is called the scramble.

When you're tired of playing regular jacks and want to play different games with jacks, some people call these different games CHEATINGS. They call them this because in many of them you do all of the things that you're usually not supposed to do.

BACKSIES is one of the regular Cheatings games. Another is the one in which you touch the jacks as you play! After you scramble them, you toss up the ball, pick up a jack and touch another jack with your finger, and then catch the ball. Then you put the jack in your other hand. On the next toss pick up the jack you touched before, touch another, catch the ball. Transfer the jack to the other hand. On each toss you have to pick up the jack you touched last time. You go on the same way, through Onesies. On Twosies you have to touch the next two jacks you're going to pick up, and so on. This game, in addition to touching, includes Carts before Horses. That is, when you're on Threesies, you pick up one first and then three, three, and three. It's a game that's all backward.

Other Cheatings games are many of the different games already given, like Double-Bounce, Cherries in the Basket, No-Bounce, and Pigs in the Pen. Then there's another that's like Pigs in the Pen except that you make a kind of tunnel out of your left hand instead of a pen, and you throw the jacks all the way through the tunnel instead of just into it. Where they land on the other side is your scramble for the next time, if you haven't missed. This takes a little practice so that you get them all the way through the tunnel, but don't scatter them too far.

PATS is a game that's fast and fun. After you've tossed out the jacks, you toss up the ball, pat the floor with the same hand, pick up a jack, and catch the ball. Then put the jack in your other hand. Each time you toss up the ball you have to pat the floor before you pick up a jack.

KNOCKS is similar. You toss up the ball, pick up a jack, and knock on the floor with your knuckles and then catch the ball. Each time, you knock on the floor after you pick up the jack and before you catch the ball.

And then, of course, there's DOUBLE PATS and DOUBLE KNOCKS.

Lots of rules are given in this book for different games and different ways of playing jacks. But often other rules are made up, and they can be good rules, too. The only thing to remember if you make up rules is that everyone playing at that time should agree on them *before* the game begins. They can't be made up in the middle of a game. And then everyone should stick to the rules. It isn't a game, otherwise.

Book Five

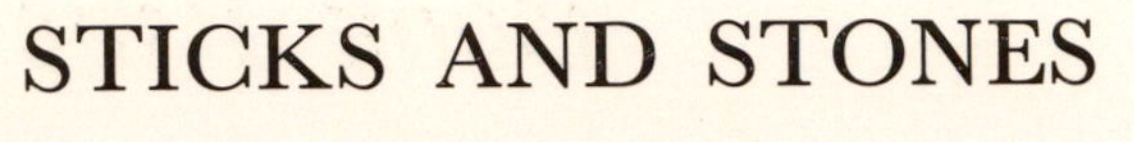

STICKS AND STONES

Sticks and stones
May break my bones,
But names
Will never hurt me!

The rhyme which begins this book of taunts and teases is a good answer to any tease or any name-calling. And I think that before telling you the teases I have collected, I will give you the answers to them.

I'm rubber and you're glue.
It bounces off me and it sticks on you.

Liar, liar,
Your pants are on fire,
Your nose is as long
As a telephone wire.

I'd rather be that
Than a brat like you.

These next two are used to someone who's staring, usually at you:

Rubber neck
Stretch it.
Throw it up
And catch it.

You can stare.
I don't care.

And, of course:

Nyaa! Nyaa! Nyaa!

can be an answer to almost anything, although it isn't very special.

But there are always more teases than there are answers. A funny way to find out if your friend is a "good child" is this one:

A good child, a good child,
As I suppose you be,
Never laugh or smile
While I tickle your knee.

When children start kindergarten they often hear

Kindergarten baby
Sitting in the gravy.

and:

Kindergarten baby
Born in the Navy.

or, a longer version:

Kindergarten baby
Stick your head in gravy
Wash it off with bubble gum
And send it to the Navy

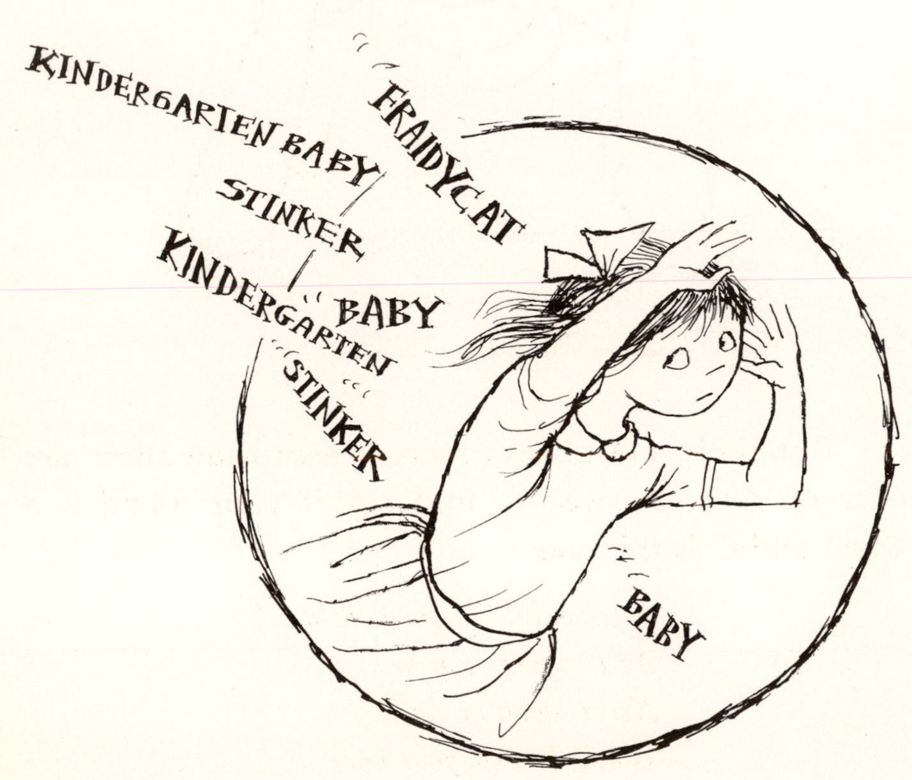

Those, as well as most of the others, are sung or chanted instead of being just plain said. This is very important to make them sound right. They are used by first-graders; after the first grade one either ignores or helps the kindergartners. The next two are sung by the third-graders:

First-grade babies,
Second-grade bums,
Third-grade angels
Eating sugar plums.

or:

First-grade baby.
Second-grade cat,
Third-grade angel,
Fourth-grade rat.

For the last day of school:

No more pencils, no more books,
No more teachers' dirty looks.

One more school rhyme, and then some to use in a game when someone's IT, such as tag or hide-and-seek.

School butter,
Chicken flutter,
Rotten eggs
For your Daddy's supper.

Judy's it
And got a fit
And don't know how
To get over it.

Nancy's it and had a fit;
Can't jump over the ash pit.

Hey, hey,
Can't catch me.
I'm sitting on top of
The Christmas tree.

Hey, hey,
Can't catch me
'Cause I'm sitting on Grandpa's knee.

Cat's in the cream pot
And can't catch me.

Cowardly, cowardly custard
Eat your father's mustard.
Catch me if you can.

The next rhymes are used when your friend is wearing the color mentioned.

Brown, brown,
You're a clown.

Green, green, you're a queen.
Soak your head in gasoline.

Blue, blue, you have the 'flu.
I don't want to play with you.

Pink, pink,
You stink.

Black, black,
Sit on a tack.

White, white,
You're getting married tonight.

Red and yellow,
Kiss a fellow.

And four of the old roses-are-red kind (you'll know more).

Roses are red,
Violets are blue.
Vinegar's sweet
Compared to you.

Roses are red,
Violets are blue.
Your head is shaped
Like a B-22.

Roses are red,
Daffodils yellow.
You are the one
Who stoled my fellow.

Pansies are small,
Tulips are tall,
I've seen some jerks
But you beat them all.

The next group of teases involves two persons. One asks the questions and the other answers, or does what is asked (up to a certain point)—and then the asker has the final thing to say, if the other person has given the right answer. As you see, some use only words and some use actions as well. The last one in this group hurts, and should be done only to friendly grownups, if at all, as most people treat others as they are treated.

Question: What comes after 79?
Answer: 80.
Then you say: You're a big fat lady.

Question: What is your favorite color?
(The other child can answer any color, but suppose it's blue.)
Question: What's your favorite number?
(Suppose the answer is four.)
You then say: You'll have four blue children.

Do you want a dollar?
Yes.
Take off your shirt and holler.

Do you want a nickel?
Yes.
Go suck a pickle.

Look up.
Look down.
Your pants is falling down.

Look up.
Look down.
Look at my thumb.
You're dumb.

Did you get my letter?
No.
Oh, I forgot to stamp it.
(And you stamp on your friend's foot.)

Guess what?
What?
That's what!

Inchme and pinchme went out in a boat.
Inchme was drowned and who was left?
Pinchme.
(And then you can pinch your friend—he asked for it.)

Do you want a penny?
Yes.
Go kiss Jack Benny.

Did you put on the television set yesterday?
Yes.
How did it fit?

Similar, in that they need answers, are the "just like me" games. If you say the first line, you ask the other person to repeat one phrase each time:

I went into the house.
Just like me.
I went up the stairs.
Just like me.
I went into a room.
Just like me.
There I saw a monkey.
Just like me.
(Or, suddenly, Just like you!*)*

This is for someone who tries to play a trick on the second of April:

April Fool has come and past,
And you're the biggest fool at last.

Many of the teases have to do with how we look, color of clothes, tallness, smallness, fatness, and how we act. Many of these are used when they *don't* really mean anything, too. And more of these are sung than said. To the tune of the *wedding march:*

Here comes the bride,
Big, fat, and wide.
Look how she wobbles from side to side.
Here comes the groom,
Skinny as a broom,
He'd wobble, too, if he had any room.

To the tune of *Happy Birthday:*

Good morning to you,
You belong in the zoo.
You look like a monkey
And act like one too.

Gingy, gingy gout,
Your shirttail's hanging out.

Captain Thirty,
Your face is dirty.

When you are old
And think you're sweet,
Take off your shoes
And smell your feet.

Fatty, fatty
2 by 4
Can't get through
A 10-foot door.

or:

Fatty, fatty
2 by 4
Couldn't get through
The kitchen door.

Caroline is so small,
A rat could eat her, hat and all.

Jane, Jane
Tall as a crane.

Tip top tower,
Tumble in an hour.

Blue-eyed beauty,
Do your mother's duty.
Brown eye,
Pick a pie,
Turn around and tell a lie.

Tattle tale, tattle tale,
Hanging on the bull's tail.

Cry baby, cry,
Stick your finger in your eye,
And tell your mother
It wasn't I.

Helen's mad
And I'm glad
And I know how to tease her:
A bottle of wine
To make her shine,
(Or: *A bottle of rum*
To make her dumb.)
And a cute little boy to squeeze her.

To cut someone down to size:

You're good! What's your name?

When a newcomer joins the group:

At ease, disease.
There's a fungus among us.

Or you can say:

Two's a couple,
Three's a crowd,
Four on the sidewalk
Is not allowed.

If someone's staring:

Take a picture. It'll last longer.

When a person copies you:

Monkey see,
Monkey do.

If a person doesn't know where to sit in an auditorium:

It makes no difference where you sit.
The man in the gallery is sure to spit.

And now a tease, a dare, and then two strictly California rhymes. To explain: in California, Stanford and the University of California at Berkeley are rivals, always trying to beat each other in football and other sports. And in California coastal cities there are fleas!

I saw you in the ocean,
I saw you in the sea,
I saw you in the bathtub,
Oooh! Pardon me!

Here stand a post.
Who set it there?
A better man than you,
Touch it if you dare!

Berkeley rides a white horse
Stanford rides a mule,
Berkeley is a gentleman
Stanford is a fool.

Lamp-lighter, lamp-lighter,
California flea-biter.

But there is a big difference between those sticks and stones you say or sing for fun, and those mean ones when you really mean it. Only you—and the one you tease—will know.

You're not really bad,
You just smell bad.

When you finish eating an apple you call:

Apple core,
Baltimore,
Who's your friend?

Someone answers with the name of someone else near, and then you throw the apple core at the person named.

And finally:

Scairdy cat, scairdy cat,
Don't know what you're looking at.

Postscript for Parents and Others

Children are the most conservative of people. In their relaxed, unsupervised playtimes, they sometimes come out with phrases or verses dating back hundreds of years. While they have occasionally learned these from grandparents, they have usually learned them from children just a few years older. Since a "generation" of childhood playtime is scarcely six to eight years in duration, this transmission is real and direct and still vital, with few if any forgotten words.

However, modification does occur with the introduction of timely characters or events. Sometimes these "moderns" are retained for a very long time. E.g., "The Spanish Dancer," "The Lady with the Alligator Purse," etc. (Was The Lady with the Alligator Purse the same person as The Lady from Philadelphia? Both are legendary American figures, household intruders full of common sense.)

Collecting this lore of the child has been fun and has led me on and on, in schools, playgrounds, streets, parks, playing with the children as one of them, the main difference being my notebook and pencil. They are the source although I have been discouraged when a child has occasionally cited one of my paperbound booklet collections as an authority. I have been perpetually encouraged by the letters I have received from them full of appreciation.

This book is about and for, and really by, ordinary, normal children, most of whom are between six and twelve years of age. Everything contained herein is direct from the oral tradition of these contemporaries of ours, unlike many books of children's games which are largely derived from older books or from adult reminiscences.

To some grownups, the information in these pages may seem unimportant, to others sadly lacking in the richness of the "good old days," and perhaps to a few even slightly vulgar. Any vulgarity seen in these rhymes or games by adults is unknown to the children who use them. Then, too, there are those who believe that children are so interested in television and other ready-made time-passers that they have lost their traditional lore. This is far from the truth and could be believed only by those who are not observing children.

Children are the carriers, preservers, and transmitters of a rich heritage and are its competent authorities and defenders. That this branch of folklore has been infrequently collected is partially due to a lack of interest in and understanding of it; sometimes to a difficulty of communication between different age groups.

Children may find this book fun; at least it has been written primarily for them and of them. Parents and teachers (and aren't we all either one or both?) may find a further understanding. Folklorists will understand that all of this material is "here and now," recorded in the oral tradition, and each example given is gathered from more than one informant.

INDEX